NATURE'S MYSTERIES

CRYSTALS

HEATHER MOORE NIVER

Britannica
Educational Publishing

IN ASSOCIATION WITH

ROSEN
EDUCATIONAL SERVICES

Published in 2017 by Britannica Educational Publishing (a trademark of Encyclopædia Britannica, Inc.) in association with The Rosen Publishing Group, Inc. 29 East 21st Street, New York, NY 10010

Distributed exclusively by Rosen Publishing.
To see additional Britannica Educational Publishing titles, go to rosenpublishing.com.

First Edition

Britannica Educational Publishing
J.E. Luebering: Executive Director, Core Editorial
Mary Rose McCudden: Editor, Britannica Student Encyclopedia

Rosen Publishing
Shalini Saxena: Editor
Nelson Sá: Art Director
Michael Moy: Designer
Cindy Reiman: Photography Manager
Sherri Jackson: Photo Researcher

Library of Congress Cataloging-in-Publication Data

Names: Niver, Heather Moore, author.
Title: Crystals / Heather Moore Niver.
Description: First edition. | New York : Britannica Educational Publishing,
 in association with The Rosen Publishing Group, Inc., 2017. | 2017 |
 Series: Nature's mysteries | Audience: Grades 1-4.
Identifiers: LCCN 2015047447| ISBN 9781680485837 (library bound : alk. paper)
 | ISBN 9781680484878 (pbk. : alk. paper) | ISBN 9781680484564 (6-pack :
 alk. paper)
Subjects: LCSH: Crystal growth—Juvenile literature. | Crystals—Juvenile
 literature. | Crystallization—Juvenile literature.
Classification: LCC QD921 .N58 2017 | DDC 548.5—dc23
LC record available at http://lccn.loc.gov/2015047447   4-18

Manufactured in the United States of America

CONTENTS

WHAT ARE CRYSTALS? 4

SHAPES AND COLORS 8

HOLDING IT ALL TOGETHER 10

GROWTH FROM SOLUTION 12

FROZEN SOLID 14

MELT WITH ME 16

GORGEOUS GEMS 18

CHAMELEON CRYSTALS 20

CRYSTALS IN THE WORLD 22

CELEBRATED CRYSTALS 24

GROW YOUR OWN CRYSTALS 26

GLOSSARY 30

FOR MORE INFORMATION 31

INDEX 32

WHAT ARE CRYSTALS?

A crystal is a certain type of solid object. It is a form of matter. Scientists describe matter, or everything that can be seen, according to the way it is made. All matter is made up of tiny parts called **atoms** and molecules. If all those parts are arranged in a regular repeating pattern then the object is a crystal. The outsides of crystals have a regular pattern of flat surfaces that meet in sharp corners.

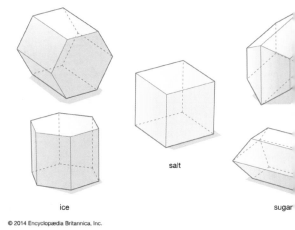

ice

salt

sugar

Different substances form different crystal shapes. But all crystals of the same substance have the same shap

VOCABULARY

Atoms are tiny particles that are the basic building blocks of all matter. Atoms can be combined with other atoms to form molecules, but they cannot be divided into smaller parts by ordinary means.

Most solid matter that is not alive is made up of crystals. Common substances such as sugar and salt are made of crystals. So are metals such as gold, silver, copper, and iron. Diamonds, emeralds, and other gems (precious stones) are also crystals. Some objects are not made of crystals, however. Glass is one such example. Its molecules are not arranged in any particular pattern.

Crystals include lovely precious stones, also called gems, such as diamonds and emeralds.

Matter exists in several different forms, called states. The three most familiar states are solid, liquid, and gas. Matter in a solid state has a set size and shape. Those do not change easily. In the liquid state, matter has a set size, or amount. However, its shape depends on its container. For example, milk changes shape when a person pours it from a carton into a glass. But the amount of milk stays the same. A gas does not have a set size or a set shape. It can expand to fill a larger container or can be squeezed into a much smaller container.

Phase changes of matter

gas

sublimation

deposition

evaporation

condensation

melting

freezing

solid

liquid

The states of matter include solid, liquid, and gas. Matter can change from one state to another, such as by freezing or melting.

THINK ABOUT IT

Many crystals behave like butter. They are hard at low temperatures but turn soft at higher temperatures. Why do you think that is?

Most crystals form when a liquid changes to a solid. Water freezing is a familiar example of this process. As water freezes, its molecules line up and join to form ice crystals. Snowflakes are collections of ice crystals. Crystals also form when a liquid with matter dissolved (melted) in it dries up. For example, when salt water dries up, salt crystals form.

A snowflake is made up of a collection of ice crystals. Each snowflake is different, but most have six points or six sides.

SHAPES AND COLORS

The way a substance's atoms or molecules are joined together creates a crystal's shape. The arrangement of atoms in a crystal is called a **lattice**. Crystals form in many different shapes. However, all crystals of the same substance have the same shape. For example, salt molecules join together in a cube shape. Therefore, salt crystals are cubes. Sugar crystals are column-shaped and slanted at the ends. Quartz crystals are six-sided columns.

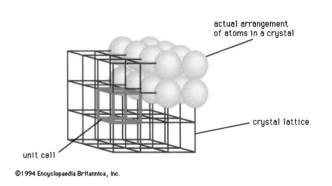

actual arrangement
of atoms in a crystal

crystal lattice

unit cell

©1994 Encyclopaedia Britannica, Inc.

This image shows a typical crystal lattice. The arrangement of atoms in a lattice creates the shape of each crystal.

A lattice is the arrangement of atoms or molecules in a crystal. A lattice is three-dimensional and repeats.

Most minerals are crystals. Minerals make up Earth's rocks, sands, and soils. Some of the most common minerals are metals—for example, gold, silver, copper, and platinum. Diamond, quartz, sulfur, mica, talc, and salt are other well-known minerals. Minerals come in many different colors. They also reflect light in different ways. The luster of a mineral describes how the mineral appears as it reflects light. Some minerals are transparent, or see-through. Others are iridescent, which means that their color changes as light hits them from different directions.

Minerals come in a wide variety of colors and shades.

HOLDING IT ALL TOGETHER

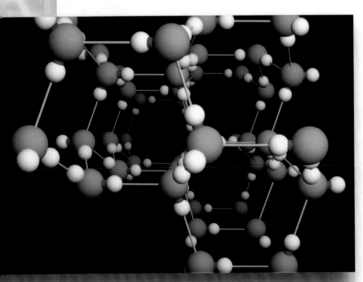

This computer-created model shows how the bonds of an ice crystal hold molecules together.

Atoms and molecules in crystals are held together by bonds. Bonds are formed when particles called electrons from one molecule interact with another molecule. There are different types of bonds. Some crystals are held together by just one type of bond. Others are formed by a mixture of bond types. Different combinations of bonds form different repeating patterns in crystals. A crystal's appearance depends on what types of bonds hold its atoms together.

The bonds within a crystal determine its properties. If the bonds are strong, the crystal will only melt at a high temperature. If a crystal is made up of weaker bonds, the crystal will melt at a lower temperature. Weaker bonds can also cause a crystal to be more easily reshaped.

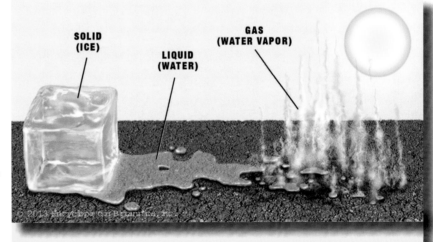

The bonds between water molecules are different in the different states of matter.

GROWTH FROM SOLUTION

Crystals need just the right conditions to grow, or crystallize. One method for growing crystals is called growth from **solution**. It is the easiest way to grow large crystals at home.

A solution of saltwater, for example, can be made by mixing table salt with water. The table salt will dissolve, or break apart into particles that mix evenly with the water's particles. If the solution is left to sit

A crystal forms in this solution of sodium acetate. This crystal is sometimes called "hot ice" because heat is released as it crystallizes.

VOCABULARY

A **solution** is a mixture of two or more substances that stays evenly mixed. Substances that are combined to form a solution do not change into new substances.

uncovered for several days, the water will evaporate slowly. This means that it slowly turns to a gas and floats away. When it does, the salt particles come together to form crystals. Many crystals, such as amethyst and fluorite, can form this way naturally underground. Sometimes crystals are created as hot water cools deep inside Earth.

A single salt crystal looks like this up close. When table salt and water are combined and the water dissolves, salt particles join together as crystals.

FROZEN SOLID

Have you caught a snowflake on your tongue? That was a crystal! Crystals often form naturally as a liquid changes to a solid, such as when water freezes. As water freezes, its molecules join together in a regular and repeating pattern to form ice. Snowflakes are collections of tiny ice crystals. The speed at which the

Water can exist as both a solid (in ice form) and as a liquid, depending on the temperature.

water cools or freezes determines the kind of crystal that is formed. Snow, ice, hail, and freezing rain are all ice crystals. Ice crystals can form in minutes.

Some crystals are formed out of thin air! Snowflakes grow from water molecules in the air all the time. When the air has more moisture in it than it can hold, it is **supersaturated**. All this extra water changes from a liquid to a solid as it crystallizes.

When the air contains more moisture than it can hold, the water can crystallize into a snowflake.

MELT WITH ME

S ome crystals form from magma, or melted rock found deep inside Earth. The sizes of the crystals that are formed depend on how fast or slowly the magma cools. When magma cools quickly, small crystals form. Magma that cools slowly forms large crystals in the rock.

Magma inside volcanoes and the lava that volcanoes emit both cool quickly. These liquids form the rock found in Earth's crust near its surface. This rock contains tiny crystals.

Rock formed from lava that cools quickly contains small crystals, such as these blue Hauyne crystals.

COMPARE AND CONTRAST

How is crystal formation affected by temperature? How is it affected by time?

Deep underground in Earth's mantle, however, magma can cool much more gradually to form rock. The rock in Earth's mantle has much larger crystals inside of it. These crystals may take many years to form.

Diamonds are crystals that form about 100 miles (160 kilometers) below the surface of Earth. They form at very high temperatures. Diamonds that are found on Earth's surface have been brought up from below by magma and volcanic eruptions.

Diamonds are crystals that are created under conditions with very high temperatures. They can be many different colors.

GORGEOUS GEMS

Most gems are hard minerals that are found naturally in the earth. Like most other minerals, gem minerals are crystals. They can vary greatly in size. Some gems are huge blocks weighing many tons. Other gems are tiny specks that can be seen only under a microscope. Rock crystal, a common gem material, is found in chunks large enough to be carved into massive vases and plates. The crystals of chalcedony are so tiny that for a long time, people did not think they were

A pearl is just one example of a gem that is not a crystal. Can you tell by looking at it why that is?

COMPARE AND CONTRAST

How are crystalline gems such as diamonds and rubies similar to noncrystalline gems such as coral and pearl? In what ways are they different?

crystalline. There are some gems, however, that are not crystals. For example, coral, pearl, and amber are noncrystalline gems.

The rarest and most valuable crystalline gems include diamonds, rubies, emeralds, and sapphires. These gems are all transparent, or see-through, minerals. Diamonds may be yellow, pink, blue, or black. Rubies are red and emeralds are green. Sapphires may be blue, violet, yellow, green, or almost black.

Sapphires are extremely rare and valuable crystals that may also be many different colors.

CHAMELEON CRYSTALS

The lizards called chameleons are best known for being able to change the color of their skin quickly. They can do this because they have tiny crystals inside their skin!

This relaxed panther chameleon's skin contains miniature crystals that reflect light and seem to change color to blue.

A chameleon's skin has two layers that are made up of **cells** that contain crystals. A chameleon changes color by stretching or relaxing its skin. This causes the crystals within the skin to move farther apart or closer together. When

Cells are tiny units that are the basic building blocks of living things.

the crystals move, the colors of light that are reflected by the crystals change. For example, the tiny crystals within a chameleon's skin reflect blue light when the chameleon's skin is relaxed.

A chameleon's skin changes color for several different reasons. A male chameleon's skin, for example, will change color to attract a female or warn off another male. Its skin will change from blue to white, from green to yellow, and from red to a brighter red in just minutes.

This panther chameleon's skin contains crystals that help it get attention by changing to bright red or other colors.

CRYSTALS IN THE WORLD

Many crystals that are very beautiful, such as diamonds, are also very useful. Diamonds are valuable and the hardest mineral in the world. Though they are prized for their sparkling appearance in jewelry, they are also valued for their usefulness as tools, such as diamond saws. Diamond-tipped tools can cut through granite rock as easily as a steel saw cuts through wood!

A clear mineral known as quartz is another kind of crystal.

Tools such as the blade of this saw contain hard diamond crystals, which can cut through granite.

THINK ABOUT IT

Many televisions have liquid crystal displays (LCDs). Liquid crystals are not actually crystals. They have some properties of liquids and some of crystalline solids. What might cause a substance to have properties of both a solid and a liquid?

It is one of the hardest minerals. When electricity is sent through a crystal, it vibrates. With quartz crystals, this vibration is so exact that they are often used in watches. The regular vibration keeps the hands of the watch moving at exactly the right time. Crystals are also used in many electronic devices such as computers and cell phones. Solar cells, which convert the Sun's energy into electrical energy, rely on crystals, too.

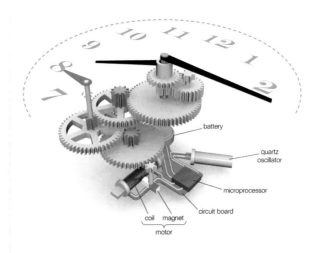

This image shows how a quartz piece fits with other parts of a clock to help watches keep time.

CELEBRATED CRYSTALS

Some of the world's largest crystals are found in Mexico's Cueva de los Cristales (Cave of the Crystals).

Mexico's Cueva de los Cristales (Cave of the Crystals) has enormous crystals! Some of the world's largest crystals can be found 1,000 feet (300 meters) below Naica mountain. Some are as large as 36 feet (11 meters) long and weigh up to 55 tons. Until 2007, scientists puzzled over how they were formed.

The crystals grew so large because the conditions under the mountain were just right for them to grow. They grew in water that had a

THINK ABOUT IT

Under the right conditions, crystals can grow to any size. What conditions do you think can limit how big a crystal can grow?

lot of minerals. The temperature of the water didn't change much. It was the right temperature for a mineral found in the water to continue to dissolve and form a crystal called gypsum. Crystals kept growing because the conditions in the cave did not change. Eventually, the crystals grew to the size they are now. Closer to the surface, at about 400 feet (120 meters) deep, a cave called the Cave of Swords has walls studded with crystals that look like swords.

The Cave of Swords gets its name from walls that are covered with sword-shaped crystals.

GROW YOUR OWN CRYSTALS

Humans can now make crystals by solution and other methods. Synthetic gems require various types of equipment.

For a long time, crystals were only found in nature. Early in the 19th century, scientists began to experiment with making gem crystals themselves. In 1902 August Verneuil of Paris started the first commercially successful process for making gems.

Natural gems and human-made gems look the same to most people. However, an expert can tell a human-made gem by physical differences. Gas bubbles are

THINK ABOUT IT
Sugar is a common household item that you can use to make crystals. Can you think of any other items at home that might work?

sometimes found in human-made gems. Natural gems, however, have bubbles of liquid.

You can grow crystals in your own kitchen! Here's a growth from solution method good enough to eat. You'll need a piece of string, a tablespoon of sugar, a glass bead, a small jar, ½ cup of hot water, and a pencil.

- stick
- string
- jar
- saturated solution of sugar in water
- starter seed

© 2010 Encyclopædia Britannica, Inc.

Using this type of setup, you can grow your own sugar crystals at home.

Slowly stir the sugar into the hot water until it no longer dissolves. Now you have a saturated solution.

Thread the string through the bead and tie a knot at the end. Tie the other end to the pencil. Place the pencil across the top of the jar opening. Let the string hang down inside the jar. The bead should weigh the string down into the solution. However, the string should not touch the bottom of the jar. Leave the jar and string undisturbed for about a week.

As more and more sugar is stirred into hot water, it will stop dissolving. The solution is now saturated.

If a crust develops on the solution's surface, break and remove it carefully. This will allow the water in the solution to continue evaporating.

Eventually, cube-shaped sugar crystals should form on the string. This is rock candy!

Crystals shaped like cubes will form on the string, and you will have rock candy!

GLOSSARY

CONVERT To change from one form or use to another.

CRYSTALLIZATION The process of changing into a solid form that is made up of crystals.

DISSOLVED Broken apart and evenly mixed into another substance.

GEM A natural substance found on Earth that is valued for its beauty and often used in jewelry. Most gems are hard minerals found in the earth. Others come from animals or plants.

LUSTER A shine or sheen produced from reflected light.

MINERAL A naturally occurring solid crystal found in the earth that does not come from an animal or a plant.

PROPERTIES Special qualities or characteristics of something.

QUARTZ A common mineral that is often found in the form of a hard crystal and that is used especially to make clocks and watches.

REFLECT To move in one direction, hit a surface, and then quickly move in a different and usually opposite direction.

STATE A physical form of matter or anything that takes up space. The three most familiar states of matter are solid, liquid, and gas.

TRANSPARENT Able to be seen through.

VIBRATE To move (or to cause something else to move) back and forth or from side to side with very short, quick movements.

FOR MORE INFORMATION

Books

Dorling Kindersley. *Rocks and Minerals* (Pocket Genius). New York, NY: DK Publishing, 2012.

Hoffman, Steven M. *Gems, Crystals, and Precious Rocks* (Rock It!). New York, NY: Rosen Publishing, 2011.

Pellant, Chris. *Rocks & Minerals* (Smithsonian Handbooks). Revised. London, England: Dorling Kindersley, 2010.

Tomecek, Steve. *Everything Rocks and Minerals* (National Geographic Kids Everything). Washington, DC: National Geographic, 2010.

Zoehfeld, Kathleen Weidner. *Rocks and Minerals* (National Geographic Kids Everything). Washington, DC: National Geographic, 2012.

Websites

Because of the changing nature of Internet links, Rosen Publishing has developed an online list of websites related to the subject of this book. This site is updated regularly. Please use this link to access this list:

http://www.rosenlinks.com/NMY/cryst

INDEX

amethyst, 13
atoms, 4, 5, 8, 9, 10, 11

bonds, 10–11

Cave of the Swords, 25
cells, 20, 21
chalcedony, 18
chameleons, 20–21
crystals
  how to grow your own,
    27–29
  shapes of, 8–9
  uses for, 22–23
Cueva de los Cristales,
  24–25

diamonds, 5, 9, 11, 17,
  19, 22

electrons, 10

emeralds, 19
evaporation, 13

fluorite, 13

gas, 6, 13, 26
gems, 5, 18–19, 26
glass, 5
gypsum, 25

ice, 7, 11, 14, 15

lattice, 8, 9
lava, 16
liquid, 6, 7, 14, 15, 16,
  23, 27
liquid crystal displays
  (LCDs), 23

magma, 16, 17
metals, 5, 9

minerals, 9, 18,19, 22,
  23, 25

noncrystalline gems, 19

quartz, 8, 9, 22–23

rock candy, 29
rock crystal, 18
rubies, 19

salt, 5, 7, 8, 9, 12, 13
sapphires, 19
snowflakes, 7, 14, 15
solid, 4, 5, 6, 7, 14, 15, 23
solution, 12–13, 27–29
sugar, 8, 27–29
supersaturated, 15